Remember When We Defeated Goliath

~A FAITH BUILDER~

R.O. ROCHE

DEDICATION

Firstly, to God and my Savior Jesus Christ who is the main "Lighthouse".

To my wife Marlene and my son Jorge Roberto who have "dazzled" my life.

CONTENTS

ACKNOWLEDGMENTS

I thank Marlene because she was on the alert for every detail of my book, that only somebody with such sensibility and intelligence could advice.

I thank my translator Myriam Padrón, for helping me in making this book real and possible in English.

I also say thanks to the painter, Javier Dueñas, who gifted me his valuable art so that my book has a cover.

And to my brother Alain and my cousin Reinaldo, for their encouragement.

Thanks to all those who in one way or another one, have given importance to my humble book and what I have to express.

FOREWORD

Thanks to the Grace of God I met R.O. Roche, a young man blessed by Christ's beautiful blood, who fights in the Power of the Holy Spirit to remain victorious in this Hard fight, that all the believers who want to exalt and glorify the name of Christ face.

By means of an exchange of Christian matters, one day the result of a prodigious pen was available to me and reached my hands as evidence of a skilled and talented mind which had been provided by God.

His writings were inspiring, his thoughts were rough, grievous and truthful expression of the reality of those who fight and shed tears to give Christ the first place in their lives because they have understood that He in His Grace and Mercy shed His blood and offered His life to give to all of us eternal existence.

When reading our dear Roberto's words, there is no doubt that they are the result of a soul redeemed by Christ and even when suffering tremendous victories and defeats, he knows how to express sincerely and with transparency what our Saviour is able to make.

i

Today, these meditations have been of tremendous encouragement and comfort for us because we live in a convulsed world managed by the forces of the wicked ones who walk as roaring lions that look for someone to devour but that at the same time, such meditations have an intense and deep desire of making Jesus Christ be the target and the full governor of our lives.

I encourage all of you to be part of this beautiful work that I hope it will fill your everyday lives with blessings and it will be considered as inspiration to be a luminary in this world that is about to disappear.

Pastor José Mallén Malla

Pastor since 1982 in the Church Convertidos a Cristo, Santo Domingo, Dominican Republic.

Author of the book "Romanos", de la serie Bosquejos Comentados para Predicadores (Editorial Portavoz).

Ministry "Compartiendo Bendiciones" through Internet.

UNFORGETTABLE CHRISTIAN REFLECTIONS

Some years ago I wrote a series of stories. I wrote them without thinking about publishing them, much less to share this set of stories with so many people; I only experienced that with my closest friends and some relatives.

Little by little those stories were increasing, not only in number but also concerning the amount of personal feelings and creative and fancy options that were able to get out of my own heart. Then a Pastor from the Dominican Republic, who placed on me his confidence, prayers and support, encouraged me to continue writing them, with the fact that they could be good to help others.

My life was full of sadness. I could see people everywhere receiving apparently undeserved miracles, but my miracle seemed to be completely impossible, without understanding that a miracle was also happening to me. The sort of facts that I was waiting for, events of the past thought to be dead that could revive again in the present, never really happened, but outstanding things did, so I could change my life and see many other good things.

Then, one day I gathered all those stories into a book which I entitled *"The Lighthouse of Asaph"*, because I like lighthouses a lot, and the name of Asaph due to a man of the Bible who was sad and discouraged. That biblical name had been engraved on my mind when one night one of the young people of my church came to visit me accompanied by others. He wanted to encourage me spiritually and used an illustration based on Asaph. I used to visit lighthouses of Cuba and made reports for pleasure; and as the lighthouses are generally associated with the guide of Jesus for us, I made the decision to use that allegory.

Every year, when arriving the terrible and threatening hurricanes of the Caribbean, I lose sleep and the happiness, fearing that the strong winds could pull up the trees that my father planted almost forty years ago; some of them are already rootless, but there are still many in foot and this fact is one of the best memories that I have of him. Many times my mother and I were praying next to the door while the wind blew irresistibly outdoors. When I think of something like that, I also imagine that our faith can be considered as trees which are looked after by other people, new ones can be planted as renovated reasons and good actions and ideals to be fed, comparable with lovely kept seeds of those old demolished trees. A new way to rescue the faith from the mean of the pain that exists around us may be thought as well.

Many times my memories and thoughts transformed into dry leaves, then they were gathered as ashes, but one day, miraculously, all those ideals began to hold testimonies, varied texts and memories that could be good for others to begin again. It was not a simply personal game of learning how to use words but of reviving myself when using them.

JESUS

There is nothing sadder than to ignore the best and the most beautiful thing that exists and that will exist. For that reason, Jesus reigns in my heart and though I am unworthy, I always have an unconditional friend who forgives my iniquities.

In the saddest moments, when tears come to my eyes, He reminds me that I will never be alone and that I can hold on firmly to His shoulder. His word is an endless spring, and a parchment that never ages.

He is who laughs and cries with me; He is who rejoices at the happiest moments of my life as well as who makes my small advances in life become news where The Father is. He has a young heart and is always ready to be my shield, the face that appears not only in the crowd but also in solitary and dark places, He is who picks me up when I do not even want to get up. He is such a priceless hug that heals my heart.

Though I feel hopeless and lost, Jesus is constantly cheering me up, He remembers me every moment. For Him, we are always his greatest achievement, His main concern. Jesus is who makes us valuable and He is who draws a smile in our lips when we only feel pain. I surely know that no matter how hard my life can be, He will never turn His back or even point at me; on the other hand, I will see His open hands offering consolation and peace.

It is sad to want more than Jesus himself, His hug of unspeakable feeling and His voice full of hope, He is able to light up each heart as difficult as it may seem. It is Jesus who touches our hearts every day, and who calms our thirst.

I never bore Jesus with my sadness and my errors because He lives to cheer up my spirit, to forgive me and to tell me what I need to listen to. When He calms my thirst I feel that He also cures my wounds. His word is perfect because when He speaks to me everything makes sense.

That is the smile that I want to portrait all my life, the person that I want to feel knocking on my door. I want Him to be the visitor who is seen when descending on the way to my house. I know that once, He died for me, and eternity will live to give continuity to my life.

And there are more things to say but I just have to mention: Jesus.

THE HUG OF DAVID

Returning to my "world", this Sunday morning, I hugged the Bible in my room; I lifted it with my hands, while I prayed and my heart groaned full of regret and desolation. I had not even touched it for an extremely significant time.

Now, the beatings of my heart and my sadness tell me that I need a hug, a prodigal son's hug, a hug of angels who take care of their children. Maybe the redeeming hug of the Lord for David, who after collapsing in pain due to the consequences of his sin, humbled and cried until the unspeakable thing.

I want that comfortable hug that only God can give me. I need the restful waters and the green grass that my Pastor preaches. My upset and confused soul needs the end of my pain for years and the light that is missing from my life, it is not that of a home, not even that of the Sun, it is the transparent and calm peace of the Lord.

David is returning to the Lord, he is remembering Goliath's times, his victories and his great blessings of the past. However, this time he prays from the bottom of his heart, for the mercy of that God who made him King, and who blessed him when he was a simple and insignificant shepherd.

I discover how important humility is in the things that come from the Lord when a longsuffering prisoner, who is Christian, fills me up with hopes in his letters but hundreds of people surrounding me are not neither able nor want to to do such things.

The Lord is good. He remembers a sort of David full of errors and pain. Although the consequences of the sin are only a shade on his forehead, the Lord raises him high again and heals his heart.

God, remember when we defeated Goliath, when we pastured sheep or we threw, in vain, the nets, and You chose us. Do not remember neither our iniquities nor our transgressions, throw them away at the bottom of the sea. Do not allow us to become drowned in water when we walk towards You, and keep us away from the perverse road so that we deny You nevermore.

If we are full of rebellions, as your people are in the desert, mercy upon us so as to accept our grievous errors and confess our sins; we need to learn the potter's precept because it is only Your hands which can amend and state our fate.

It does not matter that we feel Peter's crying or Pablo's sorrow and grief, give us the blessing that You sowed for ever in their hearts; give us the hug that You gave to David when he humbled himself before You, and once our hearts have been healed, we could be able to give them to others as well. Give us the miracle of being touched by Your hand again.

O LORD, you have searched me
and you know me.
You know when I sit and when I rise;
you perceive my thoughts from afar.
You discern my going out and my lying down;
you are familiar with all my ways.
Before a word is on my tongue
you know it completely, O LORD.
You hem me in—behind and before;
you have laid your hand upon me.
Such knowledge is too wonderful for me,
too lofty for me to attain.
Psalm 139

DINNING WITH THE LORD

I have wandered over the streets at nights looking for somebody to talk to. Some nights have been dark and a drizzle has made my clothes humid. Sometimes, the Christians who have always encouraged and advised me have already gone to bed; their houses are dark and silent; then, without bothering them and being a little sad, I have followed my way and I have headed to mine, then, I have attempted, by means of the prayer, to have an encounter with The Lord.

I imagine that it is a night of surprises; I am having dinner with The Lord. There are neither inhibitions nor protocols; The Lord is in front of me, and despite I feel His presence and Himself so familiar, my whole being is full of a great joy that I had not felt before. I do not even have any desire to complain about something, I simply feel His presence in my life, and it is the greatest and only miracle that I need in that moment.

A happy day is not common; it is as a clearing in the sky amid a storm, it is as an oasis in a desert. The Bible does not make a lot of honor to the word *happiness,* even to the word *happy*. It is easy to notice that as incredible as it might seem, there are more important and durable things that have to do with the joy and the experiences of obedience and worship to the Lord.

I would like my happy day full of human events. I would like to go through all the stages of life which may show me that I am alive, that I have accomplished all my goals, and that everything goes well in a general sense. But due to all my experiences, I have realized that God has a better concept and plans about my happiness which are demonstrated in expressions of His love, and they have another meaning and influence in my own heart. Although those human experiences are still important for me and I wait for them with faith, I keep on searching happiness in other things, close to my brethren, trying to discover what implies being a servant of The Lord.

I also try not to focus only on myself. I try to discover what would give joy to others; I also try to offer something that sometimes has no meaning to me but maybe it will fill someone else's heart with joy because a currency reaches a higher value in a hand of someone who needs it or in a grateful heart although this currency has no real value for most of the people.

Every day of our Christian life is a happy day, it does not matter if we feel sad and surrounded by tests and adverse circumstances. We are quiet only because God is in us, and we have the promise of eternal life in our heart, which yearns all the benefits of the faith. Then, we are willing to give a word of encouragement to somebody, we pray for our brother, although we are undergoing tests and worse necessities. We assist the brethren who seem cold and down because they will lift us in the future.

It was one of those dark nights in which I needed to speak about my problems with any brother, and when I was heading home feeling all frustrated, I found a missionary friend in somebody's front porch. It was summer, and a seasonal rain was falling; there was no electricity and he patiently expected a transport to return home in another town.

It was an immense blessing to stop and talk to him about my tests, to share our thoughts, our experiences of a Christian life and the things that please God to see in His sons and daughters. I felt as if I were having dinner with The Lord that night but it was much more beautiful and significant to imagine, to feel and to be sure that The Lord prepared everything for me. That was merely a happy day in my life, and I was no longer sad.

Jesus replied: "A certain man was preparing a great banquet and invited many guests. At the time of the banquet he sent his servant to tell those who had been invited, 'Come, for everything is now ready.'

"But they all alike began to make excuses. The first said, 'I have just bought a field, and I must go and see it. Please excuse me.'

"Another said, 'I have just bought five yoke of oxen, and I'm on my way to try them out. Please excuse me.'

"Still another said, 'I just got married, so I can't come.'

"The servant came back and reported this to his master. Then the owner of the house became angry and ordered his servant, 'Go out quickly into the streets and alleys of the town and bring in the poor, the crippled, the blind and the lame.'

" 'Sir,' the servant said, 'what you ordered has been done, but there is still room.'

"Then the master told his servant, 'Go out to the roads and country lanes and make them come in, so that my house will be full. I tell you, not one of those men who were invited will get a taste of my banquet.' "
Luke 14:16-24

THE PERFECT STORY

They wanted the "perfect" story, without miracles and without churches, so that sin did not seem so bad neither the Christians so good; where the suffering one, the abandoned one and the ordinary one did not count any story. A story to give meaning to the vanity of the World and to open the doors equally to all the experiences.

They wanted clearly understood, the reason why evil covers and overcomes good so easily; the reason why the man who has abandoned his wife can hardly remember her affection, her tender cares and her love without measures; and while she is thinking that she is present in his mind, she is for him only a vagrant and uncomfortable memory that never appears in the most meritorious moments of the day.

They wanted a story full of peace and harmony; with a God who does not abide by all His promises; and with many children who claim not to believe in Him; but with capable men who are willing to substitute Him with their songs.

They intended a story of long roads without shades, all of them built by man's hands and with the blood of others, they also intended to step on the grass without noticing the dead butterflies; that the forbidden fruit would be a trophy, and the mantle of iniquity that human beings take inside would be similar to their own freedom.

They imagined a story where sinners and their blasphemies were applauded and fully accepted because there are always new rights to conceive. A story of new experiences, without prodigal children, which never forgives the past, and follows a new road without looking backwards. A story where errors did not count and they were taken as lived experiences.

They wanted a story without tears or pain, without cancer, without thorns or angels.

They wanted a story without me, without my brethren, without regrets or redemption; besides, a story without Heaven

They wanted a "perfect" story, without Psalms, a Godless eternity, but they only had the story of The Saviour who died in the cross of the Calvary, and they did not really like that story very much.

THE DRAFTS OF SAMSON

"... and they tied him with chains so that he could mill in jail."

Judges 16:21b

Samson had a draft in his life that he had not finished writing. Now he worked very hard in the mill inside his prison cell, and his life was stemmed as a result of sin. His rigorous punishment, turning and turning every time, denoted the deep damage that the fact of disobeying God can cause; creating a vicious circle "sin… consequence."

Samson resisted Satan for a long time, but missing several of the most important votes like nazareo, unfulfilling the will of God, and after being deceived by his enemies, now he was the toy for the Philistines. A long conspiracy and a simple deceit of a woman had transformed him into a defeated and reduced Samson concerning all the aspects of his personality. All his previous challenges had reported him victorious routes but his existence seemed to fail totally.

Samson is not so distant from our lives; God wants us to learn from him.

Many times Satan becomes people into cloths and at the same time, they are made toys of the world. Then, the good purposes become unconcluded drafts. Tears are not enough to express the defeat and humiliation. Hands are full of all those drafts, and it is only possible to make a clamour to God for the true and genuine restoration of a life in ruins.

Repeatedly we use the inkwell and our fingers have many vestiges of ink, but anything gets to be official; we do not show it to people or purposes merely stay on the table; then we have to address our steps and to meditate about ourselves. Maybe we have many ideas and feelings that we want to revert in benefit of the testimony and our siblings' communion or maybe our life needs a miracle that we move away every day with our facts and outrages.

Then, let us look for the will of God. Samson achieved it blind and broken-hearted. After being humiliated and being felt lost, he requested another opportunity, he recovered the initial purpose of his life and it was forever reflected in the Word of God. He had solved to transform his last draft into a memorable end.

If you are a man or woman destroyed by a great circumstance or you are a Christian who has an unconcluded draft, you can request for the power of the Holy Spirit to take out your life from the lurch. Do not notice the days of glory of Samson so much, when he loaded the heavy doors of the city or when he easily revenged on the Philistines; it would be rather to look at when he was turning the heavy wheel, burnt to ashes while God prepared him for recovering his dignity before Him. His last draft was already finished.

When suffering is quite long, it is widely needed to follow the will of God. It is difficult to achieve it but every thing that is pleasant to God can be reached.

"Then Samson prayed to the LORD, "O Sovereign LORD, remember me. O God, please strengthen me just once more..."
Judges 16:28

SAND IN MY EYES

Looking for an independent, comfortable and easy way of being Christian, somebody decided to believe on his own way, according to the events and daily reasons of his life. He would simply pray from time to time, amid the problems and necessities, and maybe he would read the Bible when he would experience pleasure indeed in doing it. This person would believe in God like all the other ones but remaining as a free thinker "of duties and useless formalisms and commitments". Then, he should not be "an expert of the Christian faith", but "a correct man, of good spirit and will."

This man found the way very soon and he felt pleased with it because whatever thought he had, God would be waiting for him at the end so he missed his Church, that one he would not visit any more. Hence, as he could not accept absolutely anything that takes him out of his new way, he impeded in his thought any doubts in that sense, becoming quickly deaf of hearings anything which attempts or varies his new decisions. This human being was obliged to escape from and avoid the company and the sibling's word of faith because there would be always a person with goodness in his heart, who would show him the truth with love.

Every day he intended to change and be a man of an extraordinary existence but his independent faith only settled down for him a plaintive and bent church of a single man so devoid, remote and gloomy that to say at times "I am now with God", it could only be possible by means of his persistent and mistaken stubbornness.

He always dreamt spiritual goals, but a feeling of despair and distress persisted night and day, at any time, and even in dreams so as not to be able to feel that joy that he abandoned and even forgot.

His new Church seemed to be amid an insane desert. And there he was; at the expense of living a suffocating day or the coldest and unbearable night; surrounded by walls almost destroyed and by strange and absurd objects. And in his eyes, there was always sand which the incessant storms spread into the air.

After wandering for a long time, his reality was more and more painful because for him there were not any enjoyment, love, peace, nor faith but whatever he had never asked for him. And what is the idea of believing if the demons were also very sure of the existence of that God they tried to face every day inside the man?

Without bearing this, that one accepted to be the loneliness and sadness as a helpless suffering in order to remain, from now on, without faith or value to face life. And the uncertain fact was at his feet, for which one day, it would be necessary to return there, over the abandoned way, just where he lastly stepped.

What kind of Church is this one, where nobody can remain because there will be sand in his eyes?

A RED SEA FOR A LIFETIME

There is a Red Sea which lasts for a lifetime. It is a long itinerary and it is used to be called "life of Christians." The world considers it a ponderous cross, quite difficult to handle.

Moses is not physically present, neither many of them can be seen around but The Lord is the patient and constant guide. He is who gives that strength that is manifested through the redemption and the new road when man's effort is already finished.

It seems to be that there are no speedy horses that go ahead, neither cars loaded with soldiers of the Pharaoh. At certain moments, nothing seems to be worthwhile but a miracle is constantly thought.

It is evident how Satan has prepared everything to destroy the hearts; that his calendar does not have blank spaces neither canceled dates; and that although someone no longer listens to the energetic screams coming out from the throats of the hosts of men, there is a song of hope that is reaching when the most difficult and urgent moment of life has just appeared.

There is a Red Sea for a lifetime when we face those terrible and difficult tests that seem unfair and humiliating; that are considered as nightmares that do not end, and that turn forces against the heart when a solution is needed even more.

That is the reason that even if we give the back to God, He does not abandon His care about us and His hand keeps apart water amid the most intense and incomprehensible pain.

He shows us that if everything is dark and uncertain, it is because we are going through a tunnel; and later on, there will be fulfilled purposes, and it is beautiful and healing the light which awaits at the end of the test since the goal is already prepared ahead of time.

The Lord knows that one day, someone will be reborned from the ashes and the new horizon, that has always been waiting, will be discovered.

The life of the Christian is difficult and valuable. Tears and pain are not few, neither the moments that inspire doubts and take him to the most heinous discouragement.

That is why, there is a Red Sea so that we can cross it for a lifetime. A Red Sea that does not cover up the hearts but it would rather take them to the presence of The Lord through the dry land...

Then Moses and the Israelites sang this song to the Lord: "I will sing to the Lord, because he has won a glorious victory; he has thrown the horses and their riders into the sea. The Lord is my strong defender; he is the one who saved me. He is my God, and I will praise him, my father's God, and I will sing about his greatness. The Lord is a warrior; the Lord is his name.
Exodus 15:1-3

SIMPLY THE BEST

God! You know how to be on my best behaviour as well as how to understand me; You are my Father who traces my life and gives me the mercy that makes me live one more day. The enemy tries to catch me in a trap in my road but Your luminous path guides me safely through all them.

Your presence and love are light from all points of view because there are no shades in you; I only receive what is good and healer that takes me to you. Every night when going to bed, my heart has a miracle and the coming dawn tells me that You will never abandon me.

My Lord, I appreciate Your guide a lot because when I do not see future events in my life neither I am motivated towards next happenings, You place the eagle in the sky so that I can look further and feel my being to be renewed.

I also have to thank You because You push Your Spirit inside me, and that makes me feel the fineness that can be found in what is truly pure.

Father, the enemy does not want me to trust, he wants me to feel that anything is worthy while and anything is true. However, You make an exception for everything and You preserve a rock in my road so that it can calm my thirst; You have a rainbow that reminds me Your promises as well as a careful provision that as doves of the sky may change my state of spirit.

You are the strong hand that takes me when I am in the air and I feel that I am falling, then Your words are the best inspiration I have ever heard. The main reason to thank You is simply to live the goodness or misfortune of my everyday life and to notice Your will behind all of us.

And if all my plans are ended in order to change my life and if I no longer see any signs, You simply make me think of You and begin again.

Thou art my hiding place; Thou shalt preserve me from trouble; Thou shalt compass me about with songs of deliverance. "I will instruct thee and teach thee in the way which thou shalt go; I will guide thee with Mine eye."
Psalm 32:7,8

THE FRIENDSHIP'S SECRET

(The following article is based on the friendship's eternal essence)

One day, many years ago, a young man wanted to make an insensitive and boring joke. He made his best friend keep for some time, something that did not have any importance and he also made him think that it was something greatly valuable, likewise he could also appreciate or test his curiosity and faith because he doubted about much human values.

He took a small cedar coffer and he placed a mocking note inside. Some small metal and wood pieces were good to give the coffer certain weight and a sort of an interior enigmatic sound. Not to make the fact of curiosity so difficult, instead of a padlock, he tied it firmly with a rope. Any discovery would be noticed at once in his friend's face, whom he knew since he had the age of discretion.

To confer honors upon "good theater", an autumn afternoon he gave the entangled coffer to his friend, keeping the jeer for a coming day. The young boy who received the charge held the coffer very carefully and went walking through the park. But due to all changes of life that would become, he kept the coffer for many years.

The small coffer traveled through three continents; the man saw battle fields, floods, big snowfalls and he could feel the saddest or happiest moments for a human being. This man ended up losing half of his family, and all his belongings more than once but this coffer was the most important object in his life and he took care of it with the greatest zeal.

So years passed by, and the young man of this story ended up forgetting the joke and the coffer. Both men aged and the coffer continued in good hands but it should be returned to its original owner. So, the old man with the coffer, sick and moribund, called the close person he trusted in, his oldest son, and made him swear he would fulfill the mission of returning the coffer to his best friend.

When the old man with the coffer died, his son made a long trip and he could finally find the original owner of the small coffer. This old man who walked in front of an old building got widely surprised when seeing the young boy with that coffer in his hands, and at once he remembered the joke with great sorrow

He was given the following note which was next to the coffer:

"My good friend, I have left this coffer zealously under my son´s care. Although I have been with me for a lifetime, you have never been a blame for me. I cannot take care of it any longer but believe me that it has been an honor to serve you and that you have trusted in me. Maybe it seems to be incredible but many times to keep your valuable secret gave sense to my life;

you allowed me to look towards future time with hope and you made me feel important. So, what is it more outstanding of giving worth than the fact that a friend trusts in another friend? Thanks for being my best friend."

The young bearer of the charge felt deeply apprehensive, he could not undergo his feelings, and he asked the old man:" What a great secret was it which deserved that my father had kept it with him for all his life, during all his tribulations and misfortunes?"

The old man, with his voice interrupted by the emotion, could only hit upon to answer: *"the friendship's secret, that is worthy a lot."*

Then the disturbed old man turned back and left crying down the street while he hugged the small coffer as if the object would disappear suddenly. And he kept the coffer without opening it until the day of his death.

He who covers over an offense promotes love, but whoever repeats the matter separates close friends.
Proverbs 17:9

A friend loves at all times, and a brother is born for adversity.
Proverbs 17:17

A man that hath friends must shew himself friendly: and there is a friend that sticketh closer than a brother.
Proverbs 18:24

THE MIRACLE OF THE TIME

He walks through life opening all the doors that he could not find before. Today he thinks of the miracle that, from the hand of God, can bring the time; he thinks of the difference of those years that passed clamouring for something like that. He wanted something urgent for his life, however, he just needed some time.

He can see his children playing in the same place where he used to spend some sad hours, thinking of the things he did not have. He visits the same hospital where he lost his dear human beings, only to fill up others´ hearts with hope and maybe he does not know them well. He shakes hands and asks for forgiveness to people that he offended or hurt at some time. Some of them do not remember, but he feels at ease.

When he can notice his great current blessings, he feels that they all come from the sadness of his youth. God used them so that the earnings and benefits would be bigger and he could see all his life, everything as a masterpiece resulting from wise hands.

Things that happened when he was trying to look for a way out, sometimes not even with so much interest and own will, were considered as the entrance door for all the happy events. No longer tears in those places of the past, neither full thoughts of sorrow. He realizes that, although he is full of memories, everybody has taken a place to bring into harmony his life and present time.

Good things he wanted to learn with more interest were the less important ones, and everything that people did not want to know, now can be noticed as the target of his life and his greatest blessing.

He is pleased in seeing other young people when they are trying to look for a solution for their problems and they realize the same thing that he does. Sadness seems to drown them, and they feel so impatient and sometimes seemingly devoid that once more, he feels that they have taken the proper road as he did...no matter how difficult it seems to be.

Now he has patience to see the ships move slowly, instead of walking along the streets looking for something he even knew. He does not get lost any blessings because he has learned that he has to wait for them in the correct place; in the port of life: handed by God.

His children and friendship learn from him because he is an open book. He feels already prepared to meet his God. It was only necessary the faith and the miracle of the time.

...who through faith are shielded by God's power until the coming of the salvation that is ready to be revealed in the last time.

In this you greatly rejoice, though now for a little while you may have had to suffer grief in all kinds of trials.
1 Peter 1:5,6

THE LAST SHEEP

Everybody has someone who humanly seems not to be redeemed or saved, and to whom smashing facts would not supposedly follow: the last sheep that makes joy not being complete and then, awakes a strong feeling and blame in the heart.

We live in a church that is enjoyable in the presence of the Spirit. Due to the careful hand of God and the blood of Jesus Christ, we can see the souls to be redeemable. Enlivening brings those brethren who were distant and cold into a place where the clamour does not seem to be heard.

Our heart is moved emotionally when seeing one of those faces which was absent because we were also absent for some time. All brethren feel great apprehension for a sheep that has returned to the fold; maybe it is a relative, a friend or a stranger; in truth it is already considered as a fact and a blessing.

When we see the redemption of somebody, we also think of others who need it; and we also remember and feel there is a sheep that seems not to return.

What will bring back that brother? Will the prayer day by day in our thought and mouth be? Will the faith that there is always a light at the end of the day be? Maybe the perseverance? Will the smashing fact of any event in his life be? Have we ever said to him the last word or phrase? Will that last word or phrase we have never said to him be? Let us think and feel that there is not any sheep completely lost, and God bears all of them in mind.

A last sheep will always exist, for that reason every day we stop at the door and we look as far as possible. We imagine that the sheep arrives and stays by our side when we no longer waited for it.

We think that our brethren and dear human beings are still very far and they will never arrive in our fold but it could happen that due to tears in our eyes, we could not see they are coming along the road. Let us keep a place for them because the answer to our yearning will be an example of the power of God.

The last sheep when being absent removes patience and dreams from us but when returning, our hands are risen thankfully and our lips express: "Jesus, if there is a 'last sheep for us' there is also one for You and You never forget it"

Who must wait for the last sheep but that one who loves it more? Let us go with Jesus who always awaits for His sheep, even the one that does not seem to arrive.

"I am the good pastor. The good pastor lays down his life for the sheep."
John 10:11

THE TRAINS OF LIFE

It was a very sad day for me. I was in the train that would take me home. Short after its departure, I could finally find a seat and I noticed that along the parallel rails, to my left side, another empty train of passengers was running and reached us. It ran quicker than ours; the locomotive seemed much more potent and it could be compared to hardness of life. It could not be otherwise, it was a superior machine and it went with an endless step. I felt very bad in relation to the hearts that you cannot reach neither change although you offer your life for it because it is already too late.

For a moment the two trains began to approach due to the shapes of the rails; it could be seen perfectly well the interior of the parallel wagon train. Then I thought "it is the moment in which these two trains will be nearer each other, no much time will pass by, and they will begin to go away again; it is similar to life; one should see the moment and enjoy it before it gets lost forever". It happened like that, a few seconds later, the trains began to go away one from the other one.

It was as the representation of the severeness of the problem that I was undergoing. That locomotive seemed unbeatable and ours was "inferior ". It had also happened the best moment, when the two trains got very close. It showed me the cold and hard reality of our existence: sad in thoughts, and painful when it happens.

But when I was still thinking upon this idea, the shape of the railways changed again and the two trains began to come closer again, maybe not to the extent of the first time but it happened again, and not only that: our machine increased its speed considerably and the other one reduced its. Our advance was touching me and maybe it would not have any importance for another person or another day; it would be something trivial but I thought of that day and it was very meaningful and remarkable to experience such fact.

At that moment, I thought: "God, in fact we do not know practically anything. It is only You who knows how our life as well as our own destination must be forged by the accidents of life and pain crossroads like the ones I feel, and in which we should start from zero in our way towards You and our path through existence."

"Many times we believe we are lost but we are not; the circumstances we believe in are not suitable but we have enough forces; concerning the dilemmas we think about laboriously, we already knew their answers. It should be enough for us that You would be in charge of things, that You are perfect and You love us as we are not even able to express in short."

"Thank you for the trains of life because when it seems that we lag behind and our moment has already passed by, in fact we are facing it and with the best steps, as You wish. Amen."

THE LIGHTHOUSE OF ASAPH

His road is as the whisper of an old man. He tries to fill it with promises so that when he gets up every morning, positive thoughts about his 36 years of existence may come to his mind. Sometimes, Satan wants him to think negatively for feeling that he undergoes the same things all over again as well as he makes no progress or walks in circles. However, though a little confused, he knows that when Christ guides oneself, there is no road without a starting point and a destination.

When he walks and sees the extreme situations of life; when he meets people who apparently rejoice without keeping God in mind, he remembers the Psalm 73 of Asaph, and how men seem to live successfully without the presence of The Lord in their lives, and then, how everything changes, and damages are clearly seen: old men's ailments and ancient things that were already announced become real.

Sometimes he feels the errors of his life are a charge difficult to forget. Some of them seem to be repeated through time and they bring him old memories of a very sad state in the past. Although this situation is no longer the target of his life, it is a thorn in his body which he tries to alleviate. The most important thing is that God keeps on telling him, in different ways, that everything is forgotten and that He wants him to begin a new life.

His road takes to an old lighthouse in the coast and to the doors of a church because amid his tears and memories, he makes an effort so that his life can be a guide to others. And though he is sometimes afraid that his light does not get anywhere, the Word of God tells him that there is no reason to despise oneself in the way he has been doing it.

He feels hopeful when somebody is blissful because of his friendship and person; he knows he is rewarded by The Lord if he receives the blessing that comes from the concern of another human being. He realizes that God rewards him, even when he no longer believes in many things and considers himself as a forgotten and defeated individual.

When he sees the gleams of light of the old lighthouse, he tries to solve some more complex and difficult things but when he is tired and sad, he puts himself in the hands of God because He is almighty and the good outcome that he needs, it will only be possible by a miracle.

And if there is a happy coincidence in his life, something impossible to explain, he asks God for reasons. Some answers and changes seem to be delayed and just the patience that comes from Him can make him await confident.

He wants to be a faithful Christian forever, and although he seemed to be far from that reality, every day he is about to make his dream come true. Feelings kept in his chest become each moment a postcard of love and hope. This fact makes up his memories and also the only treasures he possesses.

In a common day and all dressed in gray, he gives thanks to God because He showed him why sufferings sometimes transform people into human beings who are ready to be born again. He knows that God loves him, and it will be forever. He knows this love will always be real, as an eternal lighthouse: and he sees just what Asaph did.

THE ONLY PLAY

During my years of Junior High School I was interested in playing chess again, such game which I have known how to play since I was 8 years old. Without having the necessary training, I participated in a match and I was really impressed for being a "chess player."

Although my hopes, I could not enjoy my first chess match. My opponent had surprised me with a classic play that all chess players know as "Shepherd's Mate" or "Scholar's Mate". My only match had lasted some few minutes.

I stared the face of the boy who played with me; his face had a mischievous expression. That boy was smiling because he had defeated me quite fast. I could not conceive that he had won me in such a humiliating manner.

That night I was very sad when I took the bus to go home. Time passed by, and some time later, I learned everything about the "Shepherd's Mate"; I also learned some simple defensive movements to avoid it instantly.

My opponent had not forgiven my innocence; however, in a sense, I had become a better chess player.

Thinking about this experience of my adolescence, I remember, in a very especial way, a sentence that a Pastor told to my mother at a very difficult moment of her life. He said to her: "When God makes a play, it is because there is no other one that he could make". For years I have heard this statement many times as part of her speech, and I thank her because she also sowed it in my heart in the saddest moments.

Going into deeper thoughts, it moves me emotionally that God does not make it to humble or "to defeat us quickly", nor He makes it to show us that He is superior and greater than us nor that He plays at random. I cannot even come closer to think how much love can be found in His omniscience and perfection, when preparing each detail of our lives as well as when tying with delicate ribbons, each answer and solution to our dilemmas and problems.

It is difficult to accept things when they seem to be the "only play". But I cannot imagine a chess player who has taken so much consideration with us and that although we do not understand Him; when He wins, we also win. It is the only play that is made with love. It is all understood by my dear human beings and even by me.

Difficult moments will always exist but God has prepared all so that His will has a positive result in short or long terms. He does not make any movement unconsciously in His simultaneous match with thousands of millions of people. And although some things that come from His hand will be always sad, all His love and wisdom will not be absent in them.

God never plays that sad "Shepherd's Mate" that I received in my childhood. It is simply an eternal play that will save us.

MY HELMSMAN

There are thoughts and commendation reasons which are born when you pass over an ordinary bridge. It is also during a day without so much meaning, full of questions and frustrations in a general sense.

In a day like this one, it was possible for me to see that abandoned, old and almost sunk boat that remained exactly beside the bridge. The boat lacked of a significant part of its wooden frame. Although I did not want to stop, I reduced my steps because at once that shady and strange scene, in a certain way, had touched my heart.

At that moment I remembered another old ship that since I was a boy, I have seen it for years run aground in the coast. Every year the structure was more eaten away by the saltpetre, the oxides and time. Its size was smaller and less significant. Recently, I could see that there were left some iron pieces of the old structure and it could be noticed that at some time in the past, it had been a big ship. Just the old memory in my mind might give its true identity back to it.

In my long road through life, in a world where everything seems to change and to disappear, I can imagine that big ship that crosses the turbulent waters of the world which surrounds us, I can feel that Christ is the person who received me when "I was born again"; he is also my trip partner through my Christian life; who will never say goodbye to me because it will be due to faith that His arms are opened up in the celestial mansion.

He is the person that when I wake up I observe Him seizing upon the helm of my life with His safe and firm hands, and when I go to bed I trust Him my heart. I can clearly see that He is the helmsman of all my blessings.

There is something in Christ that gives me joy; it is His simplicity and authenticity, the way by which He is bound to all us and to each one of our feelings, the way by which I have the best answers, that they come clearly from His hand as well as patience and search resulting from the prayer.

In the Bible I can read the beating answers that came out from His mouth whose truth marked the final point to any dilemma or adversity. Even today those words have the same effect and nothing is better than that reality. His advice is good to encourage and build up a damaged area of our life though it could seem to be ruined. It moves me that being God so sublime and wonderful, every minute He is interceding for us and giving His love which is our greatest wealth.

When I take a promise in my hands, I feel as part of Him because Christ is as drops of dew; He lives every day among His children. He does not need to be finding out events or things since He knows all of them

He simply comes to give us hope, sanity and a transformed heart. And then, we can still navigate.

He is always picking up what seems not to care to anybody and what seems no longer to serve and He is giving to it the value of the gold. He can be found where the believer is in death agony in order to whisper His great love. He is next to the saddest and sorriest sinner that can exist to take his hand and bring him to His presence.

He is next to us, His valuable children, just to tell us that He takes the helm and we can already rest again.

Christ is surely the helmsman of what was lost before. Everyone who trusts his life to Him will be taken through the turbulent waters of this world and when awaken he will already be in a safe port.

There is no helmsman like Him!

Behold also the ships, which though they be so great and are driven by fierce winds, yet are they turned about with a very small helm, whithersoever the helmsman pleases.

James 3:4

ABANDONED BAGGAGE

Each station has its own system of regulations and specific routines for the lost and found department. Sometimes the baggage can be found in unsuspected places or in some instances, it can be found returning over its own steps. It is a simple fact: the traveler is not more interested in his belongings. Spiritually, all this has many similarities with our life, mind, even our thoughts and faith.

I had spent so much time observing a solitary old suitcase which was exactly at one of the seats in front of me. The thick leather suitcase had been all the time just there, and a lot of people tried to sit down but when noticing the baggage they left the seat free. Obviously, it was a forgotten or abandoned suitcase.

Such ideas were all in mind! When figuring out the reasons, I thought of who gives up his good purpose in life and leaves everything behind to get lost the opportunity to arrive at his goal. Furthermore, I thought of who forgot his first love to The Lord and being already in another place with a lot of concern, he makes efforts to recover it.

However, my best and more pleasant spiritual thought was addressed back to somebody who finally made his trip but time ago, and consciously, left that heavy suitcase, loaded with things that once had been closely related to him but that now, without doubt, they were hindering him and were not worth while any more; things which might have a great value but they can waste the soul of any human being.

At the end I took my own baggage and I made my trip but during the whole itinerary, I meditated a lot about each detail, much more about the spiritual sense of the person than in the suitcase or what could be found inside of it.

I imagined the moment in which that person made the decision of leaving all the old things behind and not losing his trip nor his true and real way. I thought of how blessed he should feel.

Therefore if any man be in Christ, he is a new creature: old things are passed away; behold, all things have become new.
2 Corinthians 5:17

...knowing this: that our old man is crucified with Him, that the body of sin might be destroyed, that henceforth we should not serve sin.
Romans 6:6

THE MOUNTAIN

On day I climbed up a mountain that in the distance, it did not seem to be so high. When arriving at its vicinities, I thought about small and dispersed bushes and low grazing which covered its hillsides; it was an almost impenetrable overgrowth, full of obstacles, cliffs and thorns.

On that day, our small group was so stubborn that we do not only climb up the mountain but we also climbed it down by the other side. Later, we surrounded it to return to the camp. Many years have passed by but I still have the memory of our struggle to ascend towards the summit of that mount which helps me thinking that I can reach that other goal that God affords us.

When I try to go up the mountain of life, my tears moisten the earth of its hillsides. I realize that our high mount is getting wet due to those tears; I can see a fall of souls, bent knees, exhausted brethren, some who rest from their fatigue and others who no longer can bear the test. Then I remember how many times I did not have strength to continue so at present, I offer them my hand and my word of encouragement to continue ahead. We were never told that it would be easy but Who we should trust in.

It is said that the impossible events are ended when God and the man face a mountain. I am no longer an immature young boy neither I sit down as a mountain climber full of life. The mountain seems to be much higher and I no longer think that there is a whole life to achieve the goals. Nevertheless I think that one day I will rise the high mountain of the eternal life, as high and difficult as the steepest mount but in whose summit I will cry joyfully.

I have not climbed the high mountain yet but during the process I have learned how to see the miracles that surround me. People do not even realize it but I can see them clearly enough; for instance, in sick persons who find the peace in their hearts, in those who are sad and offer the truth by means of their hands, and even in my own life.

It will always be difficult to look up and see how much it has to be waited as well as to feel the hardness and almost impossibility of the long road. Sometimes, forces are almost getting to an end. However, when arriving at the summit we will look at the mountain with other eyes and we will feel as an overcome test what we have left behind: a steep mountain that tells us every minute that our faith is not in vain while our tears go falling on its hillsides and we go away leaving our print of faith, love and hope on it.

... I tell you the truth, if you have faith as small as a mustard seed, you can say to this mountain, 'Move from here to there' and it will move. Nothing will be impossible for you.

Matthew 17:20

MY PLACE

Recently, I returned to fast with my brethren in the church. Although in my long Christian life I have only had fasts in the course of the current year; I felt that it was me again and I was coming back home. The faces of the brethren, whom I share a place with in the fast and praying group, were illuminated when they saw me rejoined to them

I really felt a little upset because the Pastor always proclaimed the stability and perseverance of the members but at a certain moment in the past, I had decided to stop fasting and I believe that his watchword, which experienced so much joy in his ministry, was affected by this decision of mine. I stopped attending the meetings of the group on Tuesdays and my individual Friday commitment.

Though he always told me that he would accept my decision of retirement as a temporary one, my place and time would be always available. At present, I get myself surprised that he never ended up discarding and criticizing me as someone irresponsible. I have realized that he really loves me a lot me and he has been my Pastor and my friend indeed.

God knew that I would return to keep on waiting for the answers I need. If in a given moment I interpreted the difficult and hard circumstances that surrounded me like a definitive decision, I was mistaken. He had not allowed me to wander about to humble myself but to perceive that His behaviour never has an end, and that His will goes across deserts and storms to make a road; certainly, I should continue waiting.

The following day I attended the worship at night. I saw an adolescent, delivering his devotional speech and with a surprising spiritual growth. Thanks to The Holy Spirit, he was most serene and master of himself. He seemed to be an older man with his short, light jacket, his hairstyle and his character. He was courageous enough to give to God what others are not able to do: to dedicate his life and youth to Him. Then, I realized how our fasting sessions helped to back up people as him.

It was not about my problems specifically nor about my life but about the life of a complete church. For a moment, I wanted to see for ever that young man and the other ones in the church; I wanted to have them steady and constant, full of their first love.

Nevertheless, I also remembered how in my individual fasts on Fridays, the biblical passages redeemed sensitive aspects of my life and they flowed as a spring, giving me advices that I have never found in other moments. They seemed to be miracles, and surely they were: the way by which I went on discovering all those Revelations so appropriate and precise and how I kept writing them in a piece of paper so finally I could write about them and tell them to others.

And maybe my life might be difficult and I have not even found the road but fasting with my brethren makes me feel hopeful and trusting again.

I believe that some day I will find all the answers, and that when learning all the things I need, God will place me in a high, dry and safe place and I will see the reason of those so puzzled circumstances that I have lived.

Then I will remember that fasts never tried to compel God for an answer but to be next to Him and to find the place perpetually kept for me.

"But even now," says the Lord," repent sincerely and return to me with fasting and weeping and mourning.

Let your broken heart show your sorrow; tearing your clothes is not enough."

Come back to the Lord your God.

He is kind and full of mercy; he is patient and keeps his promise; he is always ready to forgive and not punish.

Joel 2:12,13

LIFE OF PROMISES: AN ETERNAL BLESSING

The old woman hastens her steps to arrive at the church; she glances over her memories in her heart as well as over the different edges of her life, of her dear human beings and also that of her brethren. She has quite enough reasons to feel joyful but even the sadness is a faithful partner that brings more blessings than sorrows. She also remembers the answers of the Lord during all her life.

Ailment hardly turns off her smile when remembering those moments when she clamoured, and God showed her every year of fasting and prayers in her temple; her past life and the nights and days when she cried grievously, and when she could not even sleep or look upward because she had also missed faith at certain moments.

Sometimes, she desires to make a long list of blessings and, why not, of miracles too. Then she fears to forget something or to lose the magnificence of that feeling. She remembers all those problems, when nobody seemed to understand them, and she wrote a long letter to God.

Somebody is full of joy just by thinking that her life is a blessing and that each circumstance modeled her feelings, giving them a spiritual essence that prepared her heart to be the endearing and affecting old woman that she is today.

Her advice is so wise that encourages the spirit of the adolescent and also that of the young people who have no hope. Their tears disappear with the touch of her small and aged hands. Her speech has all the experience of life.

When she makes a promise, it is because she has lived through it, and when she gives a testimony, then we understand that she has lived the ailment many times and that the miracles are only achieved with faith, patience and love.

When still arriving at the church, she sighs and gives thanks to God. She even waits to see great miracles because she neither gets tired of clamouring for them nor abandons her faith in the divine reply.

Many brethren observe her closely and they think that one day she will go to the presence of The Lord and they will not have her pleasant company that brings them so many blessings. But then, each one understands that the Eternity is the goal, that it is necessary to discover the gift there is in oneself as well as to hold on hand to The Lord.

We still have the old woman who reminds us and she gives us testimony of a life of promises. One day she has tears in her eyes but the next day, the words that come from her heart make our own tears go away. There is nothing better to get ready for an eternal blessing than to realize that it is about to achieve the final result.

The encouragement of The Lord beats in her heart because a life of promises is an eternal blessing.

"...and, lo, I am with you always, even unto the end of the world. Amen."

Matthew 28:20

UNEXPECTEDLY

Walking around I met a merchant of success, supersaturate and weary of earnings, who gave things to the poor. He had a smile in his face. For a moment, he looked towards me and his alleviated heart could be seen. I made him an approval sign with my hand, and when following my way I could still see him in the distance taking out things from his trade, as one who thinks that anything is enough.

On one of the streets, without expecting it, I was surprised by a friend with a hug of gratefulness for something that I had made for him before; something that was not even important for me and in fact, it was not worthy. I could just say "thanks" because his expression had filled up my heart of value. I thought upon how bad and miserable I had just felt ten minutes before, but now that person who appeared to be nobody special, had given back confidence on me.

Through my way, I saw a father speaking with his son. They talked friendly and their faces were lighted by the miracle of the reconciliation. They both encouraged me to face life and I agreed with each one of their words. They knew my own problems. I remained standing in front of them and I did not want to leave, I was experiencing a miracle with my own eyes.

Near the port I met an old and thoughtful sailor who told me true stories of his life in mainland and of his small family while I was telling him my stories of lighthouses and seas that I have never seen but which drew his attention. It was a queer exchange, but we made ourselves friends and it seems that he hopes to be a Christian.

It was already late and I was coming home when I coincided with some acquaintances who attended a wedding. The bride and groom were already on the street and they moved me emotionally. I was really touched by them although I did not even know them; but before becoming sad due to the things that I do not have or I have lost, the bridegroom shooke hands with me as if he would know me lifelong. I only hit upon to say "congratulations."

When finishing the worship in the church that night, a young mental patient told me that he had prayed many times for my situation when I was distant and left home without desire of going to the church. I looked at his eyes and I found that from his innocent suffering, God was showing me something outstanding. Then I considered him as one of most important persons in the world. I could imagine him in a bench of the temple, making a great effort to remember me and all my problems apprehensively.

I also heard the sob of an old lady and of people who die everyday due to cancer. Then I looked at the sky and I prayed to God for them; but I did not stop seeing the way pointed out for each person.

Walking in solitude, I found some of the most beautiful and important scenes that beat the heart and give hopes to the soul. Others are really sad, but all of them are the ones the Lord has prepared so that we can learn from them and they can influence upon us. I could really see all that because God cares about me and He wants to show me things that are important for Him and which are constantly changing my life.

In fact, some blessings do not come from happiness or joy, but from our own problems and lacks. These are things that, sometimes we hardly request.

And it can be that the miracles that I dream of, they will never happen, but God has also known how to give me what I have never expected. I have been rewarded by Him with the great blessing of the unexpected thing.

Thanks to our Lord for all those blessings and especially for the unexpected thing.

Every good and perfect gift is from above, coming down from the Father of the heavenly lights, who does not change like shifting shadows.

James 1:17

THE CHRISTIAN RUNNER

It was a very painful year. People were not quite sure. The news was completely about natural disasters, wars, murders, robberies and countable frauds. With sadness, those of fair heart went to bed and later, they got up clamouring justice and mercy. The crops got lost due to long drought or frequent floods: dreams did not become true as they were hoped.

Deception was the common feeling in all hearts. That year, many people forgot God and just a few of them returned to Him. Each one had a sensation of living a lucky hit. It was very easy to lose the faith but very difficult to recover it.

But that year, there was a runner who was Christian and who won all his competitions without losing none of them. He seemed a miracle of God because he was never injured neither he had a head starting; as soon as the shot was fired, he ran as in a racing car and he crossed the goal line in such a way that he astonished all of us.

Amid so much pain, people always had a moment to talk about him. Then, the light did not seem deceiving and children did not fear their future. The present, that hurted as a sting, was out of thoughts when it was heard that this runner set new world records once and once again, and he greeted his people with devotion during the championships.

A lot of people talked about this extraordinarily quick witted man to cheer themselves up and advise others; he was the talk of old men and mothers. Some people tried to stain his name, saying things he did not deserve nor were they certain. However, the athlete kept on winning and it was the only good fact that happened since joyful moments were not so common.

Many people lost some of their dear human beings and properties; friends were going far away and became just memories but the runner did not disappoint anybody and it could be seen his smile which encouraged people´s feelings and heart. Humble people followed him when watching the TV programs through glass windows of the stores or when reading the newspapers; rich people wondered how it could be true that he never lost a competition and he was never absent from his place; they placed him as a sign in their business.

There was too much adversity in the world but there was a light inside that runner. He was a gift of God. That year, the runner was the best news all over the world; he was the best athlete of all.

Nevertheless, one day the runner disappeared, his followers saw this fact as something unjust in life.

Some people said that he would return and since then, they have been waiting for him everyday. From time to time, the television plays some of this athlete's images and many people come closer to God, thinking of what he could achieve amid so much pain that surrounded him just because he was Christian and God was glorified when touching each fiber of his muscles and will.

And his fans still dream that the starting shot has been fired and he is there, at the race track. The heart-stricken ones await for him with open arms in the goal line, imagining that he is Jesus. And they do not get tired of waiting his return.

I do not ask you to take them out of the world, but I do ask you to keep them safe from the Evil One. Just as I do not belong to the world, they do not belong to the world.
John 17:15, 16

A SPECIAL FEELING

Recently I underwent an experience that shocked me indeed At that moment I was already older than my father and I begun to live more than what my father could do it.

My father died due to a fatal traffic accident when he was only thirty six years old and I was hardly nine. His name was Roberto Roche; I was named on behalf of him. He was a wonderful father of an incredible will. One night, I did not hear the usual noise of the garden gate as he were coming home.

A special affection kept us together. I still remember his long walks and how he created special playgrounds for us, and made electric and mechanical changes to our toys so that they could have a better operation. He also taught me to play chess and he used to give me a present as a reward for my good behaviour. I even remember the way he scolded me. I can recall how he played with my twin brothers on the bed and how he liked to make plans about my future life. I still feel the strength of his hand seizing mine.

I have thought a lot before writing these remarks and although somebody might support an opposite statement or fact, I am sure I will see my father in Heaven. Maybe I will not recognize him as my father but he will be there, and in a certain way I will understand that there is no longer sadness or sorrow in my heart.

To cope with the sadness of a whole life, God has provided me with a wonderful mother as an angel, whose company I still enjoy. During her youth, she studied Christian Education and for all her life she has served to The Lord and to each human being whom she has met. I have never heard a rough sentence coming out from her lips targeted at somebody, on the contrary, I have only heard sweet words for thirty six years that I have lived next to her. As strange as it may seem, even to the same Christians, she has always had joy to live through the hardest tests and circumstances.

She never married again, she just devoted herself to bring up her four children, including my two twin brothers who were only two years old on that sorrowful and terrible November 18, 1979.

We never lacked of a birthday party, a picture, a pair of shoes, our clothes, vacations, trips, toys and much more than that, we have always had all her love, tenderness and the fact that Christ is the only comfort for the saddest things that may happen in a lifetime. My mother used her sewing machine from dawn to dusk to make some money for us. She sometimes took pills to keep herself awaken and not to get cut with the electric needle of her machine. Every night while we were sleeping, she worked hard without even thinking about taking any time off.

I never saw her crying. She has always been standing by, being strong enough and without thinking about her sadness, and making every effort for her children to grow in a sweet home.

She has suffered what cannot be described but she has never given her back to The Lord... It is unbelievable that even today God uses that person to give hope to my problems and my sadness. And it is my wish to enjoy my mother's company more apprehensively to the full extent of her incredible gift of tenderness and faith, as long as God allows me to have her by my side.

Through my life I have been a steady disapproval and suffering for my mother but she has only loved me much more. I know that she thinks of me as somebody very special for her. I am sure that any thing I can do for her, it will never make me feel that I am giving back to her some love and miraculous care; and though I do not consider myself as affectionate person as she is, and even though I was a child very close to my father, I believe that all what I am at present, I largely owe it to my mother: her feelings, her dedication, her love.

It is just one of my thoughts or remarks. It is number thirty six and I dedicate it to my lovely mom, Migdalia, and to my beloved dad whom I will never forget.

(Today we still live in the house built by my father and my mother for us, and it keeps on being a Christian dwelling)

ELIM WAS ON SIGHT

My Pastor prayed for me as he accustomed to do it because he is my closest spiritual consultant and he is my friend as well. I felt joyful when amid the prayer I heard him to say that I was just "at a stop in the road", that the goal would be farther on and this was not the end of all our efforts.

My Pastor also told me to get ready because after the test, great blessings would come. He made me notice that without even having the certainty of the miracle, I should already go on thinking about a beautiful day and make plans in this sense.

We remember together the Biblical passage that talks about the bitter well in the Mara desert which so much sadness and different problems brought to the town of God; we also remember how hardly people, farther on, found a desert with 70 palms and 12 wells of fresh water. We also remember Moses who had got himself ready for 40 years in order to deal with his brother, the Pharaoh. In addition, we remember José, reviled and sad who became known when he was the only one capable of understanding the dreams of the Pharaoh. The message was clear and precise: God makes things difficult so that we can know how to manage His matters properly and we can be well-prepared to receive His blessing.

I had received an answer to my prayers which was different from my yearnings and from what I considered, at a time in the past, would be a beautiful and encouraging miracle. For a moment, I felt I had been without anything in my hands. Then I ended up understanding that adversity was simply a wise answer of God, and it was only what I needed.

That day when I was at a stop in my road, I felt that I was not motivated to write; my new feeling was: How can I write if I no longer have the same reasons? However, it was the day when I appreciated what another person had said and this would bless me greatly. I did not believe to have enough words in my heart but a brother was saying them so that I could listened to them and due to them, I had a new reason to express my gratitude.

Little by little as time passed by, and maybe a shorter time later on, I discovered the right reason to understand everything: that the Christian does not have questions without answers although some of them do not seem to be "humanly" pleasant and others seem to delay a little.

I had already left the Mara desert. Elim was on sight.

Then they came to Elim, where there were twelve springs and seventy palm trees, and they camped there near the water.
Exodus 15:27

A VESSEL FOREVER

Many times I have observed the potter finishing a piece. His hands seem to be concluding the work. The vessel reaches shapes that are very attractive to me and I end up feeling that it is the form that the artist is looking for. In my mind, I imagine the final result taking into account the shape that has pleased me more; but I get surprised every time the potter presses the piece with his hands and he changes the shape of it; he moulds it a little wider or closer at the bottom probably also a little shorter; then I end up thinking that he has almost undone the work and he has lost the opportunity of stopping and realizing how beautiful it is. I notice that when the work seems to be finished, his hands still intercede taking different arrangements and varying the curves and circumferences.

The reality is the last thing I surely think: the potter is looking for the appropriate thickness and size so that the piece would not be too rough and would have the strength and necessary usefulness in turn; that it would be firm on its base when containing liquid, but being beautiful as well. He is looking for a balance among the different aspects. He is achieving a piece that lasts for a long time and that its existence would not be in vain; what he is doing is based on his vast wisdom and his knowledge of the mud, something that I do not possess.

It is beautiful and important that the Bible mentions the potter for some fifteen times in the Old and New Testament, and that it also tells us that we are like mud in the hands of God. Taking into account my appreciations, I think of the times that I have thought that I feel so good, that I do not need drastic changes in my life, in the stages of my life, when I feel so comfortable and steady that I believe not to need God to live. However, it is when God needs to change me, almost totally for me to be fine. He needs to make me more dependent on His will, more humble of heart and given to the mercy and love with those surrounding me. God wants my existence to last and not to be in vain. And it is his suppliant and merciful message which tries to rescue us from every minute of our painful condition and ignorance. He will simply achieve that we can be identified with the work of His hands like Isaiah dictates 29:16 *"will the work maybe say of its maker: Didn't he make me?"*

Through the potter's image we are shown that everything can be made new and everything can be changed miraculously. God does not want them to tramp us like rubbish mud, He would rather want us to be witnesses of the fact that every day is a miracle in His hands. No matter how we feel pressure on us, He wants the best thing for us because in such extent we will experience the fruit of His love and care. God acts in His perfect and eternal wisdom and in His exhaustive knowledge of ourselves. *"Even your hair is all counted."* (Matthew 10:30)

If we open the door of our heart, anything nor nobody will break nor crumble us like mud because God makes us new and strong in Him when we need Him. He does not make anything that it would not be miraculous, with the only end of surviving and becoming us better. God has perfect hands for the mud and for our hearts. We have our life to understand Him and transmit Him to others because we are His masterpiece which is improved every day and reaches more human and pleasant shapes at Him. We are a vessel forever.

"being confident of this, that he who began a good work in you will carry it on to completion until the day of Christ Jesus."
Philippians 1:6 (NIV)

THE MAN THAT ATE POPPIES

We met at the bus station. The idea of my trip to Havana City was to buy hardware for the computer and he was undertaking his missionary journey to San Antonio's Cape. He was an aged gentleman, and suddenly I thought he was a tourist because of his little flag and the map of Cuba.

I remember that at first, I began to avoid him but just having started our conversation, I realized that God had a purpose when getting him closer to me. I could hardly tell him about my own spiritual life. I did not want to expose so much my privacy but we could speak enough so as to understand the genuine purpose of his trip and the interesting story he was telling me.

His flag said, "Cuba for Christ" and it just turned out to be the banner of his purpose of taking the word of God from the End of Maisí to San Antonio's Cape, thus I began to perceive that mission as something tremendously enigmatic, something which could change all that seized me that morning. He began to talk about his missionary trip and how it had been from the east of the country. I did not consider that story so outstanding and important enough yet but I paid attention to him. He still looked as if he were a crazy man. At once, I became myself his "trip partner".

He began to throw upwards a currency as if it were a fleece, speaking up for probabilities because in his secular life he had been a mathematician. He suggested staying there and waiting for any means of transport. Suddenly, a taxi appeared requesting passengers to Havana, forty Cuban pesos per seat, and he rapidly rejected it since that price seemed rather high for him. For a moment, I stayed beside him ignoring the taxi but immediately I decided not to keep on with that strange company and to tell him that for the purpose of my trip I should take that taxi. However, when I got into the car and I saw him at the distance with his flag "Cuba for Christ" and other people came closer running, without hesitation, I screamed: "Come on, Mister, that I will help you!" The brother felt happy and pleased and so did I because that blessed day was about to be spoilt with my discourtesy and lack of common sense.

Once inside the car, we were four passengers. The passenger that traveled in the front seat accompanying the taxi driver began the conversation. He was also an aged-man who traveled from his distant province to Havana City, with the only idea of buying a small bicycle for his little granddaughter but he did not even know if he could find it in some store. We, the four, got out of the same bus which we had taken in different towns before, and at that moment, we were all surprised of being together inside the same taxi.

As my strange Christian brother is a sort of a person who is not ashamed of being communicative with people and likes being as such, he began to speak about his purpose of going to San Antonio´s Cape so the reasons of his voyage was the first subject of conversation in the taxi-car. I had the idea that the man in the front seat made fun of him saying things about Pinar del Río and San Antonio´s Cape, places he had visited in fact because he was a retired geologist. Later, the man told us all about his life and it seemed very sad and interesting. When he was a boy, he had to live in an orphanage without being in fact an orphan and his family after finding and hitting him hard, placed him in a reformatory. On the other hand, the taxi driver said to be a "Theologian", although he was nobody but someone full of philosophies and false doctrines who seemed to be a good person. The strange Christian brother did rebut them at the time he preached his biblical knowledge, his extraordinary idiosyncrasy and his deep Christian feelings.

During the trip he ate poppies which he had picked up in Camagüey. He seemed to me as if he were a little mad and the other ones laughed at his way of eating poppies. Later he explained the properties of these flowers but nobody already cared his so peculiar menu. The other passengers were not Christian although they said to be believers; at that moment of the journey, they were already much more on the Christian brother´s part and seemed to sympathize with his wandering life centered on the Lord.

Due to the fact that after a couple of hours the trip would end, I was already in a sad mood as somebody who does not want his vacations or the visit of his family that has arrived from a distant place to finish. We were in Havana City and the Christian brother got out of the taxi in a park. When he wanted to give me his money, half of the price of his passage, I refused it so I did not extend my hand. Actually, I had money enough in my wallet because the idea of my trip was to buy a spare piece for my computer and I thought that to pay his passage was an honor for me and the least I could do for this unforgettable man. The man was standing in the back part of the taxi and told me that the Lord would multiply what I had made for him; instead I replied that if it did not happen, it was similarly good; it was not worthy of attention.

Being at home and having my mind at rest, I am thinking and writing the anecdote at the time I wish he had fulfilled his purpose of visiting the most western end of Cuba. I never asked him if he would say some special prayer that I am sure he had in his heart or any prayer for our country, men, women and children that live in it. Perhaps, he only wanted to see the sea or the beautiful lighthouse but I feel very privileged of having collaborated in a humble manner during his trip, and that is the reason by which he will surely remember me because I perceived he is a man of excellent memory.

Some day, I would like to be able to read his own story of his missionary trip because he could tell everything with his authenticity: the places where he slept practically outdoors, each time he was hungry and cold as well as when he gave his scarce resources from the trip to the most needful persons he found on his way so the hearts opened up to Christ; besides, the treaties were distributed throughout the country. There are so many good things that there would not be space for the negative ones, and I also know that so much praise on my behalf would make him feel bad.

I felt as his brother in Christ and for a moment as a trip partner in his voyage "Cuba for Christ." That day my life was not an intermittent cursor on a white sheet of paper. Maybe people think he is crazy but God wishes Cuba for Christ, as my strange Christian brother does.

LET US START LIVING FROM HIS LOVE!

Both the visitor and that one who has been absent for a long time and returns after a long trip, present gifts to the family and friends of their lifetime; they are courteous and praise with pleasure of their dearest relatives and closest persons. To give any gift, either something material or spiritual, is an expression of recognizing the feelings as well as a sample of consideration.

The Bible talks to us about moments in which Jesus Christ, God, even the men themselves, delivered food, blessings, gifts, public positions... God gave the manna in the desert and His Son made the miracle that many pieces of bread, fish and jars of wine were multiplied and later handed out.

Nevertheless, we remember an unusual occasion when the incredibly best and fair dresses of a woman were delivered. Handing out is not always an act of kindness and love. The moment could not be more humiliating and sadder: the day of her death in the cross of the Calvary

It can be read in the Bible, in Mark 15:24: "When they had crucified him, they distributed his clothes among themselves, tossing lucks on them to see what each one would take."

Through life´s experiences, men usually behave identically among themselves. Then, they toss luck on the neighbor's soul.

I certainly know that more than once I have delivered clothings of people, condemning him in my mind and believing that nothing can still change or help him. But my finite and imperfect mind cannot understand sometimes that God has the last word for everything and this fact has been for centuries and centuries. So when we turn over ideas, then we should question ourselves as followers of Christ.

Instead of tossing luck on and condemning our neighbor, we should hug him inside ourselves and intend to help him so as to have a miracle for his life. Our lovely hand, even a simple phrase, can change the direction of a life. Jesus Christ is encouraging us to learn to give from His love, even when they toss luck on us and distribute all our belongings.

He wants us to learn from all the moments when men degraded themselves, judging the divine dignity of their son Jesus Christ and in fact what really happened was that The Lord was sacrificing His life meekly for the sake of the whole humanity.

Let us stop delivering Christ's clothes and let us start giving from His love!

A new command I give you: Love one another. As I have loved you, so you must love one another. By this all men will know that you are my disciples, if you love one another.

John 13:34; John 13:35

RESTORATION

Blessed restoration!! by which you can feel that anything or nobody can separate you from the love of God, and you become passionately fond upon yourself for all that was put aside, abandoned and unconscious, before your errors no longer care, they do not oppress your heart until crying nor they take away your dream. You do not feel that everything is lost or one more time you have tossed everything. You have peace and even though a little sad, you have thrown up yourself of your obstinacy and The Lord has come to rescue you. It did not take even one minute in giving His hand and taking you out of the well of the despair.

When everything ends up at this sad stage, I will see the greatest miracle of the world. Your peace, that is my thought every minute; your new life, that is the smile that I want to end up seeing, will no longer be my distant dream neither your future will be my spiritual charge.

There are many important questions, and although you do not know all the answers, you know which one is the kind of answers that will cause you being well. Even though the correct words are in your heart, it is difficult for you to answer in a practical way. Satan is astute, he never sleeps, he does not want you to see the light through your door. When you rest or you try to discard what moves away from God or you try to see farther than your nose and miss all the benefits, he is already preparing his next lunge.

You can touch the face of The Lord again. You believe in all those wonderful and blessed things, you have faith in the work of The Lord.

The sin will always be with easy reach because we live in rooms with piercing nails in the walls. The meat, physical and spiritually, is something with many contraindications and warnings because, in fact, it is what makes us vulnerable and the enemy knows you perfectly well.

Having been founded on the power of God and on the sentences of His children, you will reach the promises again and everything will be in the memory of those who always believed in you, and we know that, although the enemy is astute and has always fought against us, you will never lose your way and life.

It is very easy to twist the route to the darkness, to stop to be a son of the light. The first thing is to abandon the faith and believe that you are so negative, irreverent and sinful that there is no progress in your heart regarding the spiritual life that The Lord demands on you.

How recurrent it is for you to think that any good thing will not happen tomorrow but how devastating it is when you abandon the faith! What have you left if you put away what The Lord gives you to face the world and the most oppressive tests? How sad it is to believe that everything is already lost and that the miracle, the one you wait for, is something utopian and impossible!

But if you submit yourself to the Spirit of God faithfully and you hold yourself on His power all the time, allowing that He also holds you on, and receiving all His benefits and His virtue healer, you will be able to continue ahead.

One day you will reconquer what really makes you happy, you will have your own miracle which will also be my miracle.

There are many persons who surround us and need restoring although I believe that the most faithful and pleasant Christian to God is because he lives in a constant restoration. Every day, he raises his sentence like a smashed and needy man, as the publican.

You are not invulnerable nor you will never be living here. Just now, you know where your daily support is, and this is a constant incentive in your life. Everything is sensible and has a wise exit, thanks to the faith that we have given in trust to the redeemer work of Jesus Christ.

One of the best ways of knowing what is better and what is really good is to observe what others have carried out to come closer to The Lord, and what some people try to reach. At certain moments of their lives, there has been or will be the blessed trace of the restoration.

And you will claim your place again, then the miracle will be a reality because everything will have returned and you will be transparently; what I always saw.

For I am convinced that neither death nor life, neither angels nor demons, neither the present nor the future, nor any powers, neither height nor depth, nor anything else in all creation, will be able to separate us from the love of God that is in Christ Jesus our Lord.

Romans 8:38,39

ROOFS

We spend our short life building a roof but at the end, we will only see it from the Sky. I have just realized it when I was close to two persons who suffer from renal inadequacy and they are repeatedly dialyzed.

One of them was an aged-man, very kind and polite. I had taken the same taxi that picked him up to go to the hospital. At once I noticed that he was very loved by people from his town, when in one of the stops on the road, he was kindly treated by a lot of people.

Some people treated him as if everything were normal, and they requested for his services, making him believe that he was not sick. All happiness they could offer him was just to remind him his roof, that roof that he had built for his lifetime as the result of sweating blood and the honesty of his work.

The other person is a much younger woman who belongs to our church. I always become sad when I can see her red blood spots in her arm and also in her neck. They are the marks and wounded of her dialysis. But I feel joyful indeed when she stands up and speaks about her illness, her intimate and personal relationship with God as well as how she can understand the physical and spiritual process she is suffering from, and finally how she thanks to God for the things that she has learned from His heart.

The most important thing is that her faith remains; it is a sort of beautiful and true faith. I can also see her smiling, and she moves me emotionally much more when I greet her and she smiles at me without sorrow in her look.

I believe that it is needed to have a lot of value to learn the most important things in this life, to bear such a difficult test so that the cancer or another illness does not remove the truth from the heart, to think with conviction and patience when there are no much hope, and to believe that the best miracles are the ones which God gives color to.

People crowd together and they worry when waiting for another kind of miracle but they are simple and honest in the Word of God. There is a home which is always waiting; streets of gold and glass are like an image, every day much brighter in the mind of a Christian who is sick.

It does not matter chemotherapy nor dialysis; no matter that our roofs would be so important and we would not want to abandon them; that we would be sad because we have families that face hard tests; that repeated affliction would exist and seem to be all joined. It is quite difficult to understand and accept the manner by which God decides to take us to Him; even when we have dreams to fulfill.

Definitively, our roof is the love of God because the Sky is more beautiful.

It is our roof which we have been waiting for a lifetime.

The Lord made it for us, and it is the most beautiful thing He has created: our eternal dwelling.

WHAT GOD MAKES....

It is in my church where I see 6 feet tall men sobbing and shivering. It is not necessary that somebody has died and it does not care whether he was a former soldier or an academician shocked by experiences and strong emotions. I wonder how that can happen if I am simply watching an external event. God makes the lion small and His promises great.

Recently my mother was responsible for a speech on the Pastor's Day. She had her Bible opened to *2da. of Reyes 3:18*, and she repeated several times "*And this is a slight thing in the eyes of Jehovah*". While my mother was preaching, I wrote this quotation in a piece of paper because I did not want to forget it and so I could read it afterwards.

When arriving home and being in my bed, I took the Bible and I read the passage. I did not want to forget my mother's face when she repeated it over and over. She was the same person who used to sit down on the edge of the bed to cry together with me very early in the morning, almost at dawn, more than one year ago.

I have made so many errors that I get lost trying to explain them but I believe that it does not care the explanation but the love which The Lord decides with our existential bewilderment so that His will can be fulfilled. I think something like that is in the mind of those brethren, strong enough in appearance but smashed in spirit and it is also what rules the way of any Christian.

People tell me that when I finally become steady, it will already be late for many things. It is quite sad to hear that, and maybe it will end up being true. However, I really know that God is guiding my road and that one day I will smile with good reasons in my heart because God makes the lion small and His promises great.

Maybe at that time, I will not undergo these experiences which have motivated these humble texts that I have written with tears in my eyes but I will keep on sharing them so that they would not be a dead ministry but would be used as encouragement to others. It will be a beautiful memory of how The Lord transformed me and made glitter His face over all sadness and shade of raving.

All this will be possible because God makes the lion small but His promises great.

When he came near the den, he called to Daniel in an anguished voice, "Daniel, servant of the living God, has your God, whom you serve continually, been able to rescue you from the lions?"

Daniel answered, "O king, live forever! My God sent his angel, and he shut the mouths of the lions. They have not hurt me,

because I was found innocent in his sight. Nor have I ever done any wrong before you, O king."
    Daniel 6:20-22

A PRAYER FOR A WOUND

Recently the powerful hurricane Wilma almost razed the City of Havana. The wind and the strong waves attacked against the centenary levee destroying part of its structure. The streets were overflown and a lot of people were despaired due to the high level of the water that covered part of the metropolitan area and their own houses.

Some days later, my friends began to send me some photos of the tremendous flood. At once, one of them seized upon my heart. I could see the legendary Lighthouse of The Morro Castle when a gigantic wave hit the whole tower up to the highest part of it. I remembered the image of the same place which I have recorded in my mind: a beautiful place where smooth waves run towards the headland.

I felt there was no a better instance of a person who undergoes hard tests. Likewise, I believe we remember other stages of our lives when maybe we had the hands full of blessings and we did not even take care of them. These were years when we did not have concerns and griefs which put away our dreams. Then, we wondered how it was possible that we had so many gifts from God when we did not live pleasingly in His presence.

Recently I instantly thought of an exchange that, if it were carried out, my heart could sink with me. This sort of exchange would be surely pleasant to Satan.

I thought of what answer I would give if I could change my current life and return it back. I would have some things that I had lost, and maybe I could repair, perfectly well, some serious errors on time and preserve those lost things. But then, I would be discarding all my experiences of smashing and would be changing them by the past.

All my writings would disappear at once as well as the way I learned how to forgive; how I learned not to be a selfish person, how I learned to pray, even to humble and to be a better man in a general sense. I would certainly be "an occasional Christian" again and I would have unconcern again about matters of The Lord. I believe that I could not make that exchange though I died of a broken heart.

Many Christians from Havana prayed for days to see their city and their own lives return to the standard living. A short time after the flood, the pain was forgotten by means of some happy event or an answered prayer or simply due to a smile or another human being's expression. Even when people do not even notice it, the hurt always has the tendency of being restored.

The lighthouse of The Morro Castle always emitted its soft gleams. The waters had lowered at the time a prayer full of spiritual feeling and sincere heart has been answered. I could feel something special that comes from The Lord and that takes care of us and makes us trust one more day. All the tests will happen and the wounds will be restored, and one day, maybe not in the Earth but in Heavens, things will end up being much better than before.

From now on, when I feel some grief due to my wounds and my tests, I will have a new image to keep a living faith and a hope just a little steadier. Then, I will think of the old lighthouse hit by the huge wave. Amid my prayer, I will go on alternating that image with the one I have kept in my heart: a place where smooth waves beat against the headlands since positive results will always exist for our faith.

It is what is manifested and what prevails when God takes the control of our lives and encourages those who trust in Him day by day.

Because there is no wound that He cannot restored.

The disciples went to Jesus and woke him up, saying, "Master, Master! We are about to die!"

Jesus got up and gave an order to the wind and the stormy water; they died down, and there was a great calm. Then he said to the disciples, "Where is your faith?"

But they were amazed and afraid, and said to one another, "Who is this man?" He gives orders to the winds and waves, and they obey him!"

Luke 8:24,25.

THE EVIL CHEF

Satan is not considered a common chef. The recipients and crocks of his kitchen are clean and brilliant so that nobody doubts because of the appearances and premonitions. He has chief waiters and tasters who master and speak simultaneously several languages, wear neat clothes and look quiet and polite as very learned and cultivated people that they are surely. Our deceivers are the ones who tell us that our place is in the World.

The tables are majestically decorated. In a general sense, the embellishment of his restaurant is fine and faultless. The atmosphere cannot be more pleasant. Color, forms and textures sweeten the conscience and lessen the brain. There, harmony is not controversial because he has the competent and proper personnel to apply it. The word "professional" tries to be a substitute for God and the pre-eminence of what He wants for our lives.

His waiters are skilled in showing the inexplicable charms of each plate and drink that is served. They know perfectly well that the excellence that seems to offer the fullness of the world, with some fake love, causes the ties and dependences. So in this way, it is adjusted the most heterogeneous clientele never seen but totally lost for which the evil chef of this world works night and day.

The chef has a special ability to combine the ingredients of his millennial recipes. In addition, he knows how to treat a person with care.

Marriages and homes are his predilection. They receive food with the best thing they may have when leaving the oven of a chef like him. With its badge plate, the destruction fills the marriages with necessities without solution and dreams without coming true, takes away the family support and makes them face all type of setbacks and monotony. The worst thing is that a special ingredient prevents them from realizing the problems until it is already too late or it has consumed their heart and has collapsed their home. Another mysterious ingredient makes the children begin to be a problem due to their way of thinking and acting, transforming them into prodigy children of the future.

For the brethren, redeemed and born again, who face difficult tests and fight against terribly dominant bad habits and ties of the past, it is needed to find a church that helps them, and other brethren who understand them. There is also a special recipe for them: certain inconveniences so that they cannot receive the necessary support; a seasoning of fights regarding the good end of the great effort they are carrying out. In order to tinge it, a tiny piece of doubt is also required but constant and with very strong arguments, which should be prepared based on their own way of thinking of the past so that they seem to be "own solutions."

Some churches and passionless and solitary brethren, that do not thoroughly know his tricks, are considered as easy clients to attract. However, sometimes it is necessary to take advantage of the circumstances which demand for a pleasant challenge for all his personnel.

Certain fortunate ones do not return to the place never more but others are already seating for their next dinner. Unfortunately the evil chef has very good clientele because he knows the weak side of people and what would make them doubt about God and would easily remove the faith from them. His recipes seem to improve through time and the mysterious ingredients become more exclusive and varied; different dishes that hide lust and perdition are shown everyday.

Satan masters the art of persuading very well. He also makes faith seem to be distant and unconscious, and that the divine answer is an utopia that will never arrive.

If you hardly have motivation to visit your church, if to pray and read the Word are tasks which do not find a place in your daily calendar, you are already almost a client of this sad place.

He knows your weaknesses, your dreams; he knows what you are looking for in your life, those things you are fighting for so he will try to exchange your way.

The ingredients for your plate have been kept for a long time. Please, do not accept any invitation to that place!

Submit yourselves, then, to God. Resist the devil, and he will flee from you. Come near to God and he will come near to you.

Wash your hands, you sinners, and purify your hearts, you double-minded. Grieve, mourn and wail. Change your laughter to mourning and your joy to gloom. Humble yourselves before the Lord, and he will lift you up.

James 4:7-10

THE BLIND ANGEL

(The angels are perfect; they no longer have a direct and close relationship with us like in the biblical times. The following story is fiction; it is a made-up story and it only represents, to our imagination, a challenge about the miracles we wait for our lives and the way by which God can go blind through our good will)

The angel ran over the long corridors and with his hands he felt each face and shoulder. It was heard people crying, others were shouting joyfully when feeling the touch of his hands. All brethren thought that a miracle would happen, and their lives would be different and their evil deeds and wrongs would be behind.

In our short story, when somebody is touched by an angel it is as if the face were shortly lighted up. But nobody knew the reason why God had sent a blind angel to them.

The angel had touched many people as a support and relief sign but an immediate result could not be seen. People with all kind of problems stayed standing in lines or lying on the floor. They felt desperate due to their family matters, their traumas, vices, diseases and weaknesses. All and each one of them believed to be worthy of a miracle but the angel limited himself to a brief greeting or a short blessing.

People with distinct physical features, culture and age, when seeing that any extraordinary event could happen and that the angel could not see, they abandoned the place even before being touched by that angel who advanced without affording anything nor anybody specifically. He seemed to be missed and unalterable. Everybody needed God to do something with his life but any disease or deep wrong pulled up a miracle or phrase of the angel's hope. In vain, they had gone to that place.

The angel walked immutable by the corridors patiently and very methodically. Step by step, touching slightly, he stopped walking in front of a sick boy of cancer. The angel realized he had found the right person. The boy did not seem to be sick because he had a smiling face, full of peace, quite different from other people´s. The boy held on the angel in his hand as if the celestial being were the one who needed the miracle so that he would feel safe due to his own hands.

The boy kept his small hand seized firmly to that of the angel taking him among people. In his heart he had not requested anything to be changed and pleased, the truth that was untied and painless, he only delighted in seeing the joyfulness in the angel's face and he could also feel himself as a true angel. A "*gift*" given to each human being but rarely experienced.

Is anything better than a blind angel to help us to understand him?

See that you do not look down on one of these little ones. For I tell you that their angels in heaven always see the face of my Father in heaven.
Matthew 18:10

REJECTING JOB

We all take a Job inside. In smaller or bigger measure, it is possible to perceive its spiritual stature. It sometimes wakes up but due to our attitude without reasonings and lack of spirituality, it often dies rather premature. During time of prosperity, when God is hardly remembered, it seems as if it has left very far.

Good or bad moments make us feel Job from different perspectives; a sad and depressed Job, who cannot reach the peace that its soul would like to or a Job who has left a great problem behind and is able to thank God.

When there are great things that can beat us in life or we see a trail of negative consequences, we come to an agreement with God, we admit our worries and offer ourselves to a new and renovated relationship with the Creator. What is really sad about these "agreements" is that they sometimes end up vanishing together with the fog of everyday life. We cannot pay God even with our own lives because nothing is good enough inside us but it is incredibly nice to be rescued from circumstances and see the end of the storm.

At least, I remember a "pact" of my life that was good, not because the Creator´s part would not be guaranteed by means of his promises that are always made come true, since it only depends on us that a redeeming relationship would be blessed and successful. None of my hair was touched. The angels of God covered me with their wings and there was no human being doubting that His Hands were behind all things. It didn't simply seem that His Will would be hidden behind mere events and subtle ways of acting but it was rather a direct demonstration of the mercy I have implored for distressing days and nights.

I could tell a moving and long story about what happened but I know for sure you will be able to find something like that in your own lives. Something that could shake the foundations of ingratitude, the absence of devotion and the routine of our days. Everybody has any other incredible miracle in his own existence. Life is full of miracles which do not seem to be by chance.

Job has many views and contexts; you will not find something like that in social networks neither similar friends in Facebook because the big problems and sad moments make people be lack of willingness for looking through their window.

When reading Job´s story, one realizes that there are answers to many of men´s and nations´ sadness told in other biblical books and modern times.

When we see our Job dying for the lack of faith and vision, something that is called immaturity, we return to the routine of life, that way of living by which no new thing is imagined or built up to make notice the presence of the Lord among us. It is our bad habit of living one more day and leaving it to material things which do not prosper, carrying out our heavy cross that we not even call its name.

Our Job does not have a story to be told because we spend all day long rejecting it. Our Job is our biggest fear, it simply terrifies us that its sorrows and hardship could grow and increase because we consider it is a too hard shoulder to cry on.

We spend the whole life giving crutches to Job so that it can walk and its reality does not harm us a lot, for not being forced to assist it too much nor feeling its fact; not even being by its side to listen to its advice and that its example cannot upset us. Our days are going away, but our Job always expects to share something with us.

R.O. ROCHE

PHILATELY IN HARMONY

My father had a wooden petty box, as a petty coffer. Once or twice, I saw it between his hands; in one of those instances, he also showed me its content. It was his mail-stamp collection. The box was varnished, I believe that it had a sort of dustcloth in its interior that at some time, it served to put optical instruments or lab ones of his work but now it was good to save his collection.

I also remember that sometime later, being still a boy, I used to look at the shop window of the stand that formerly sold magazines, newspapers and souvenirs in the bus terminal of my town. I usually saw an album of stamps which is rarely sold nowadays, something that was expensive at that time but that my grandfather Juan finally bought it for me. He was a very indulgent grandfather towards me; he took me to fish or go for a walk, as well as he told me short stories, helping me to forget my orphan condition.

A short time later, I was already at home filling in that great album. The stamps were all drawn in black and white; the purpose was to find the originals corresponding to each place. My mother and other people took me to the post office and to the bookstores to try to find the different stamps, and with their slender economic resources, they bought me some.

I remember a married couple of the neighborhood who already died. The lady was very well known for not to return the balls that fell into her beautiful garden. In one of their trips to Havana City, they visited a privileged place for the philatelists where all the collections were sold. One evening, I was called to their house and they asked me to take the album with me. The lady, whose name was Dulce, was putting the nylon cases that contained the new stamps in each page. My album already began to be my personal pride. I stared at her caring face, full of friendlines so I forgot all the lost balls.

But one day I had the idea of going from door to door, requesting people if they had saved letters and they could give me the stamps. At that time the e-mail didn't exist, not even the telephone calls to talk to people abroad, so people communicated by writing letters. It took a long time, two and up to three months to receive a letter and many times, they were never received at the end. I could even remember when I saw those people snipping the stamps. People were different from what they are nowadays, they had time to chat and to pay attention to the dreams of a boy. Later, I submerged the stamps in water with salt to dislodge them from the piece of paper of the envelope so that no remains of the paste were left. Then, I put them to dry off inside a magazine with some thick books over it. Once, a lady gave me her grown-up son's collection.

That was the way by which I could gather so many stamps.

Although I don´t have that vast collection any longer and I lost most of the stamps through time, many others even remain. Recently, when I did not even remember that, my nephew found the album almost deteriorated because of the time and traces. He was taking out the stamps that even served and made his own collection. I felt very happy that something that I saw in my father´s life, my great passion during the childhood, could please the expectations of another boy. The past came to my mind again; that so sad stage and full of homesickness but that definitively, it is 99,99 percent of our own life.

When pasting a stamp into a letter, we hope to make somebody happy that day or to receive the appropriate answer that can supply our necessities. When recovering the same stamp and keeping it, we opt for other reasons, maybe feeling some nostalgia for a beautiful thing that can be held out, even for a longer time; moreover, trying to find out a new way in life, keeping close to the faith that better times will come. It is the same feeling that I had when simple and fond memories made me buy that album of stamps and all people by my side helped me to make my first dream true: my dream as a philatelist.

"Set me as a seal upon your heart…"
Song of Solomon 8:6

GOD BLESS YOU ALL!

ABOUT THE AUTHOR

R.O. Roche, a Christian writer from Cuba, is an internationally recognized author with stories published in English and Spanish. His book, **Remember When We Defeated Goliath**, is a story collection capturing the emotions and longings of a Cuban heart. The stories were written in an attempt to reconcile the author's life of faith with a society that discourages it. Born out of fear and sadness, sadness from praying for dreams that were never realized, **Remember When We Defeated Goliath** is a book to encourage you and help you find meaning in your circumstances.

In 1995 he won a prize for his text "Sand in my Eyes". Since 2004 his texts have appeared in national magazines of the different Christian denominations of Cuba, some cases are the titles "Jesus", "A Vessel Forever", "Sand in my Eyes" and "The Perfect Story". In the year 2009 the author intends to make his stories known internationally. That is how the English version of "The Perfect Story is published and diffused in U.S. by Living Stones News and In Touch Magazine.

Notes:

_____

_____

_____

_____

_____

_____

_____

_____

_____

_____

_____

_____

_____

_____

_____

_____

.

_____

_____

_____

_____

_____

_____

_____

_____

_____

_____

_____

_____

_____

_____

_____

REMEMBER WHEN WE DEFEATED GOLIATH